D1543169

Ecuador

by Lisa Owings

BLASTOFF! 5 READERS

BELLWETHER MEDIA • MINNEAPOLIS, MN

Note to Librarians, Teachers, and Parents:

Blastoff! Readers are carefully developed by literacy experts and combine standards-based content with developmentally appropriate text.

Level 1 provides the most support through repetition of high-frequency words, light text, predictable sentence patterns, and strong visual support.

Level 2 offers early readers a bit more challenge through varied simple sentences, increased text load, and less repetition of high-frequency words.

Level 3 advances early-fluent readers toward fluency through increased text and concept load, less reliance on visuals, longer sentences, and more literary language.

Level 4 builds reading stamina by providing more text per page, increased use of punctuation, greater variation in sentence patterns, and increasingly challenging vocabulary.

Level 5 encourages children to move from "learning to read" to "reading to learn" by providing even more text, varied writing styles, and less familiar topics.

Whichever book is right for your reader, Blastoff! Readers are the perfect books to build confidence and encourage a love of reading that will last a lifetime!

This edition first published in 2015 by Bellwether Media, Inc.

No part of this publication may be reproduced in whole or in part without written permission of the publisher. For information regarding permission, write to Bellwether Media, Inc., Attention: Permissions Department, 5357 Penn Avenue South, Minneapolis, MN 55419.

Library of Congress Cataloging-in-Publication Data

Owings, Lisa.
  Ecuador / by Lisa Owings.
    pages cm. – (Blastoff! Readers: Exploring Countries)
Includes bibliographical references and index.
  Summary: "Developed by literacy experts for students in grades three through seven, this book introduces young readers to the geography and culture of Ecuador"– Provided by publisher.
  Audience: Ages 7-12.
  ISBN 978-1-62617-174-9 (hardcover : alk. paper)
  1. Ecuador–Juvenile literature. I. Title.
  F3708.5.O85 2015
  986.6–dc23
                                                                                      2014034754

Printed in the United States of America, North Mankato, MN.

Contents

Ecuador is a small country on the northwestern coast of South America. It covers 109,484 square miles (283,561 square kilometers). Ecuador straddles the **equator**, which earned the country its name. It shares a border with Colombia to the northeast. Peru cradles the country from the east and south. Just south of the equator is the capital city of Quito. It sits beneath a **volcano** in the Andes Mountains.

Pacific Ocean waves sweep over Ecuador's western coast. About 600 miles (1,000 kilometers) offshore are the Galápagos Islands. These famous islands are also part of Ecuador. They are known for their unique wildlife.

Pacific Ocean

Colombia

equator

★

Quito

Ecuador

Peru

Did you know?

A group of French scientists journeyed to Ecuador in the 1700s. Their measurements around the equator were the first to reveal Earth's exact size.

Did you know?

Most of Ecuador is warm and humid year-round, with cooler weather in the mountains. Sometimes weather patterns called El Niño and La Niña bring cycles of flooding and dryness.

San Rafael Falls

Many different landscapes fill Ecuador's borders. The Andes Mountains run through the center of the country from north to south. These central highlands are called the *Sierra*. Many of the tall peaks are covered in snow. Several are also active volcanoes.

West of the mountains, the land flattens into the *Costa* toward the Pacific. This lowland area ranges from wetlands in the north to desert in the south. The Amazon **Rain Forest** covers the eastern half of the country, called the *Oriente*. Misty mountain forests give way to thick lowland jungle. The Napo and Pastaza Rivers flow through the forest on their way to join the Amazon River in Peru.

fun fact

The volcano Chimborazo boasts the highest peak in Ecuador. Because Earth bulges at the equator, Chimborazo's peak is farther from Earth's center than Mount Everest.

West of Ecuador is a cluster of 19 islands called the Galápagos. Volcanoes shaped their uneven landscape into rough rock piles and smooth **lava** flows. Some of the volcanoes are still active. The islands usually have dry weather. However, enough rain falls to support forests of guava trees and giant cacti.

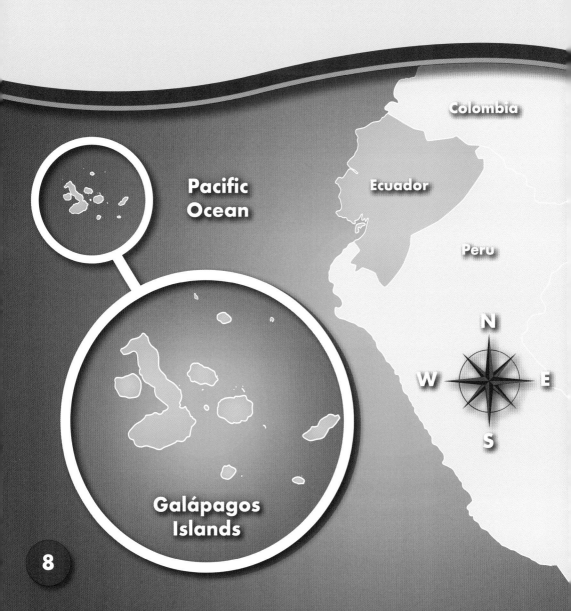

Pacific Ocean

Colombia

Ecuador

Peru

N

W — E

S

Galápagos Islands

marine
iguana

Galápagos
penguin

Charles Darwin

The Galápagos Islands are home to many animals found nowhere else on Earth. Giant tortoises and **marine** iguanas sun themselves on the rocks. Island birds include penguins and flightless cormorants. Scientist Charles Darwin traveled to the islands in 1835. He noticed small differences in the animal species from island to island. This discovery helped him develop his **theory of evolution**.

Did you know?
Ecuador's pygmy marmoset is the smallest monkey in the world. An adult is only about 6 inches (15 centimeters) long.

Ecuador has some of the world's most **diverse** wildlife. All shapes and sizes of monkeys rustle through rain forest treetops. Slow-moving sloths cling to branches. Spotted jaguars, pig-like tapirs, and small kinkajous stay well hidden in the jungle. The bright colors of butterflies and poison dart frogs dazzle visitors and warn predators.

sloth

poison
dart frog

olinguito

fun fact

A new kind of mammal was discovered in Ecuador in 2013. The olinguito looks like a teddy bear and lives in mountain forests.

The Andes are home to spectacled bears, foxes, and armadillos. Andean condors soar over the snowy peaks. In mountain forests, bird-watchers seek out hummingbirds and toucans. Pink dolphins, sharp-toothed piranhas, and electric eels swim in Ecuador's rivers. Off the Pacific coast, whales, sea turtles, and manta rays flourish.

More than 15 million people live in Ecuador. Most of them are *mestizo*. They have both **native** and European **ancestors**. A smaller mixed-race group called the Montubio lives near the coast. Other small groups include those of purely native, European, or African backgrounds. Each group claims its own identity and way of life.

Nearly all Ecuadorians speak Spanish. However, many native groups also speak Quechua or other **traditional** languages. Christianity is the main religion in Ecuador. More than nine out of ten people are Roman Catholic. Some native groups continue to practice their ancient beliefs.

Speak Spanish!

English	Spanish	How to say it
hello	hola	OH-lah
good-bye	adiós	ah-dee-OHS
yes	sí	SEE
no	no	NOH
please	por favor	POHR fah-VOR
thank you	gracias	GRAH-see-uhs
friend (male)	amigo	ah-MEE-goh
friend (female)	amiga	ah-MEE-gah

Most Ecuadorians live in cities in the Costa. Families live in small modern homes or apartments. Ecuadorians wake up early to get to work or school. They travel by bus, minibus, or taxi. People take a long lunch break, then go back to work. They buy food and other goods at large malls or colorful open-air markets.

Life is different in the countryside. Many mountain homes are made of earth and straw. Some have tiled roofs. In the rain forest, homes are made of woven palm. People get around on foot or ride bicycles, animals, or carts. They shop at local markets or gather what they need from the land.

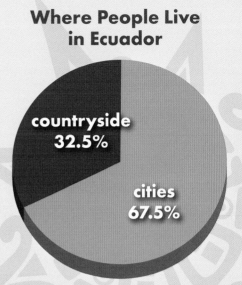

Where People Live in Ecuador

countryside
32.5%

cities
67.5%

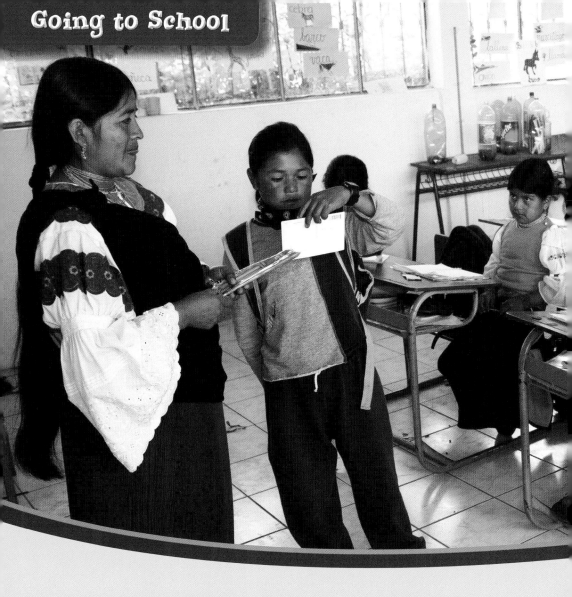

Ecuadorian children begin school at age 6. Most go to free public schools. The best public schools can be hard to get into. Classes are taught in Spanish and sometimes Quechua. Students also learn English, math, science, and history. Especially in the countryside, some students are unable to attend school. They may not have schools nearby, or their families may need them to work at home.

fun fact

Public schools do not always have enough teachers. To solve this, some students attend school in the morning. Others attend the same school in the afternoon. This way, schools and teachers can educate more children.

Most Ecuadorians continue on to secondary school. Some wealthy families choose to pay for private school. Graduates have a variety of universities to choose from. Many have respected research programs. People often travel from other countries to study in Ecuador.

Where People Work in Ecuador

manufacturing 17.8%

services 54.4%

farming 27.8%

Almost one out of every three Ecuadorians farms for a living. Lowland farmers grow bananas, sugarcane, and coffee beans. Cocoa beans are grown for making chocolate. Farmers in the highlands tend grains and potatoes. Some raise herds of cattle or sheep. Along the coast, fishers cast their nets for shrimp.

Mining oil is an important job for many Ecuadorians. Miners also dig for gold and silver. In factories, workers make food products, **textiles**, and cement. They also make wood products and medicines. About half of all Ecuadorians have **service jobs**. Growing numbers serve **tourists** at hotels, shops, and attractions. Others work in schools, hospitals, and office buildings.

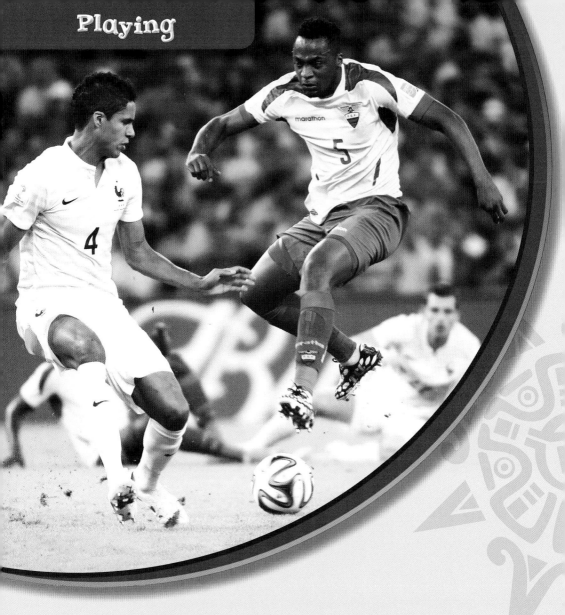

Soccer is Ecuador's national sport. Fans enjoy cheering on the national team and playing on weekends. Basketball and volleyball are other popular sports. *Pelota nacional* is a traditional game similar to tennis. Players hit a small ball back and forth with spiky wooden racquets. In *pelota de mano*, players strike a ball with their bare fists.

Families enjoy going to the beach to swim or surf. Relaxing in **hot springs** is another popular activity. The country's national parks offer hiking, mountain biking, and fishing. They are also perfect places for picnics. In cities, people often go shopping or to the movies. Young people love to go salsa dancing with friends in the evenings.

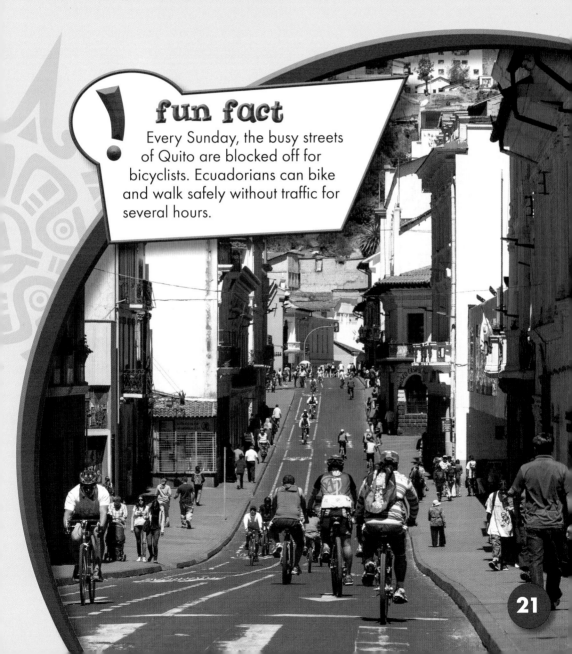

fun fact

Every Sunday, the busy streets of Quito are blocked off for bicyclists. Ecuadorians can bike and walk safely without traffic for several hours.

Did you know?

Guinea pig meat called *cuy* is a special treat in Ecuador.

Most Ecuadorians start the day with bread, eggs, and coffee. Lunch and dinner begin with soup. A favorite is *locro*, a cheesy soup with potatoes and avocado. Main meals differ by region. Potatoes and corn are **staples** in the mountains. One popular dish features cheesy potato patties called *llapingchos*. They are often served with a fried egg and pork.

Rice and beans are popular in the lowlands. *Arroz con pollo* is a common dish of chicken and rice. Along the coast, many meals feature seafood. A dish called *ceviche* is seafood flavored with lime juice and spices. Ecuadorians often get it fresh from beachside carts. Nearly every food is seasoned with chili sauce called *aji*.

fanesca

ceviche

fun fact

A rich stew of fish, squash, corn, and beans called *fanesca* is served around Easter. Some say the ingredients represent the Christian figure of Jesus and his followers.

Did you know?
Ecuador has several independence days. The city of Quito celebrates an important battle on May 24 and independence on August 10. The city of Guayaquil marks its independence from Spain on October 9.

Ecuadorians ring in the New Year by burning **effigies** at midnight. This represents getting rid of all the bad things about the previous year. Spring brings the parades, dancing, and colorful costumes of *Carnaval*. Young people take to the streets with buckets and balloons for water fights. Easter is celebrated with church services and **processions**.

Day of the Dead

Inti Raymi

Native Ecuadorians gather for *Inti Raymi* in June. They enjoy music and dancing in honor of the **summer solstice**. The Day of the Dead takes place in fall. Cemeteries are crowded with families celebrating the lives of loved ones. They make **offerings**, eat rolls shaped like dolls, and drink spiced fruit juice called *colada morada*.

Did you know?

More people used to live in the Oriente. In the 1950s, other Ecuadorians took the native tribes' land and introduced strange diseases. Many native peoples did not survive.

Huaorani

Several native peoples still follow their traditional ways of life in the Amazon. Some of the largest tribes are the Shuar, Achuar, Quichua, and Huaorani. Each group has its own language and culture. They grow, gather, or hunt for their food. Many groups rely on **shamans** for healing and guidance. Most tribes have regular contact with outsiders. However, a few choose to stay **uncontacted**.

The Oriente peoples' way of life is in danger. Logging and oil drilling are destroying their land. Tribes sometimes fight over resources. Some have turned to tourism to raise money and protect their culture. Others have banded together to save the forests. With the help of other Ecuadorians, they hope to preserve their country's precious lands and cultures.

Fast Facts About Ecuador

Ecuador's Flag

Ecuador's flag has three horizontal bands of yellow at the top, blue in the middle, and red at the bottom. Its colors were inspired by the Colombian flag and represent sunshine and wealth, water and sky, and freedom and justice. The coat of arms in the center shows an Andean condor over a mountain scene.

Official Name: Republic of Ecuador

Area: 109,484 square miles (283,561 square kilometers); Ecuador is the 74th largest country in the world.

Capital City:	Quito
Important Cities:	Guayaquil, Cuenca, Santo Domingo
Population:	15,654,411 (July 2014)
Official Language:	Spanish
National Holiday:	Independence Day (August 10)
Religions:	Roman Catholic (Christian) (95%), other (5%)
Major Industries:	services, farming, mining, tourism, manufacturing
Natural Resources:	oil, gold, silver, timber, water
Manufactured Products:	food products, textiles, cement, wood products, chemicals, fuel
Farm Products:	bananas, sugarcane, coffee beans, cocoa beans, corn, potatoes, rice, cassava, cattle, sheep, fish, shrimp
Unit of Money:	United States dollar; the dollar is divided into 100 cents.

Glossary

ancestors—relatives who lived long ago

diverse—made up of many different types or coming from many different backgrounds

effigies—models or images of people

equator—an imaginary line around the center of Earth; the equator divides the planet into a northern half and a southern half.

hot springs—areas of hot water that flows up through cracks in the earth

lava—hot, melted rock that flows out of an active volcano

marine—having to do with the sea and the plants and animals that live in it

native—originally from a specific place

offerings—items given as signs of love and devotion, often to gods or ancestors

processions—groups of people walking or moving together as part of a festival, ceremony, or religious service

rain forest—a thick, green forest that receives a lot of rain

service jobs—jobs that perform tasks for people or businesses

shamans—people believed to have a connection to the spirit world and powers of healing

staples—foods or products used regularly and kept in large amounts

summer solstice—the date when summer begins

textiles—fabrics or clothes that have been woven or knitted

theory of evolution—the idea that animals and plants gradually change over time; Charles Darwin argued that wildlife with the most useful traits survive to pass on those traits to their offspring.

tourists—people who travel to visit another place

traditional—related to a custom, idea, or belief handed down from one generation to the next

uncontacted—having no contact with the outside world in order to protect a traditional way of life

volcano—a hole in the earth; when a volcano erupts, hot, melted rock called lava shoots out.

To Learn More

AT THE LIBRARY
Banting, Erinn. *Galapagos Islands*. New York, N.Y.:
AV2 by Weigl, 2013.

Milivojevic, JoAnn. *Ecuador*. New York, N.Y.:
Children's Press, 2010.

Owings, Lisa. *Peru*. Minneapolis, Minn.: Bellwether
Media, 2012.

ON THE WEB
Learning more about Ecuador
is as easy as 1, 2, 3.

1. Go to www.factsurfer.com.

2. Enter "Ecuador" into the search box.

3. Click the "Surf" button and you will see a list of
   related web sites.

With factsurfer.com, finding more information is just
a click away.

Index

The images in this book are reproduced through the courtesy of: javarman, front cover, p. 23 (right); Ammit Jack, pp. 6-7; Boyd Hendrikse, p. 7; sunsinger, p. 9 (top); Paul van den Berg, p. 9 (bottom left); Marisa Estivill, p. 9 (bottom center), 15; Nicku, p. 9 (bottom right); EBFoto, pp. 10-11; Vilainecrevette, p. 11 (top); Dirk Ercken, p. 11 (center); Mark Gurney/ Smithsonian/Sipa USA/ Newscom, p. 11 (bottom); John Coletti/ JAI/ Corbis, p. 12; Ksenia Ragozina, p. 14; John and Lisa Merrill/ Corbis, pp. 16-17; ARCO/ Henry P./ Glow Images, p. 18; Owen Franken/ Corbis, p. 19 (left); Michael Nolan/ Glow Images, p. 19 (right); Wang Yuguo/ xh/ Xinhua Press/ Corbis, p. 20; Margie Politzer/ Getty Images, p. 21; Kristin Piljay/ Getty Images, p. 22; Ildi Papp, p. 23 (left); Stringer/ Reuters/ Corbis, pp. 24-25; Pablo Hidalgo, p. 25; Hugh Sitton/ Corbis, p. 26; Steve Bloom Images/ SuperStock, p. 27; Maisei Raman, p. 28; Bragin Alexey, p. 29 (top); rsooll, p. 29 (bottom).